Going Up

CITY SCIENCE

Marcia S. Freeman

Rourke

Publishing LLC

Vero Beach, Florida 32964

www.rourkepublishing.com

PHOTO CREDITS: Cover © Corbis; title page © Michael Connors; pages 4, 7, 10, 12, 13, 14, 17, 23 © P.I.R; page 6 © Painet, Inc.; page 11 Getty images; page 19 © James Rowan; page 20 © Armentrout; page 21 © AFP/Getty images

Library of Congress Cataloging-in-Publication Data

Freeman, Marcia S.
  Going up / Marcia S. Freeman.
     p. cm. -- (City science)
  Includes bibliographical references and index.
  ISBN 1-59515-409-4 (hardcover)

Printed in the USA

CG/CG

Table of Contents

City Buildings

Look up! City buildings reach to the sky. We call tall city buildings skyscrapers.

Some city buildings are homes. Some city buildings are stores and offices. Some are schools.

Some of us live or work in city buildings. Some of us go to school in city buildings.

How do we get *up* to the floor of our homes and classrooms? How do we get back *down* to the street?

Most city buildings have many floors or stories.

Going Up and Down

Machines help us get up and down in city buildings. A ramp is a simple machine that helps us move up and down.

Ramps and Stairs

A ramp is a flat **surface** that tilts. It **slants** from one level to another. It can be made of wood, concrete, or metal.

A ramp makes it easier for us to move from one level to another. A ramp makes it easier for us to carry something up or down.

Stairs are like a ramp with steps. City buildings have stairs that we can use to get from one floor to another.

When ramps are too **steep** for us to use, steps make it easier to go up and down. But we get tired if we have to climb a lot of stairs. Powered machines help us move up and down.

So, some stairs move! An escalator is a stair that moves. We can ride on an escalator in a store. We can ride on an escalator in a bus station or train station.

Pulleys and Elevators

An elevator is another machine to help us move up and down in city buildings, You can take an elevator to get from one floor to another. When you get on an elevator, someone might say, "Going up?"

An elevator on the outside of a building.

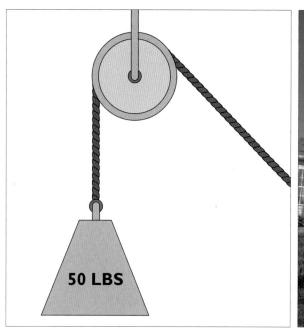

Some elevators use pulleys to move them up and down. Pulleys are wheels with ropes or **cables** around their rims. We use pulleys to help move people and things.

Ropes are attached to pulleys above.

Window washers use pulleys to move them up and down. Window washers move up and down the outside of a skyscraper.

Powered and simple machines help everyone move up and down.

Glossary

cables (KAY bul) — a thick rope made of many wires twisted together
machines (muh SHEEN) — devices or gadgets that help make work easier
slants (SLANTZ) — leans or slopes at an angle
steep (STEEP) — sloping at a big angle
surface (SUR fis) — a flat face or side of something solid

Index

Further Reading

Freeman, Marcia. *The Work Book.* Rourke Publishing, 2004
Tarsky, Sue, *The Busy Building Book.* Putnam, 1998
Welsbacher, Anne, *Inclined Planes.* Capstone, 2000

About The Author

Marcia S. Freeman loves writing science books for children. A Cornell University graduate, she has taught science and writing to students of all ages, and their teachers too. She lives in Florida, where she fishes, bird watches, and writes.